NURSING HOME BLUES

A Collection of Poetry

Radomir Vojtech Luza

Original Cover Design and Sketches by **Patricia Murphy**

authorHOUSE®

AuthorHouse™
1663 Liberty Drive
Bloomington, IN 47403
www.authorhouse.com
Phone: 833-262-8899

Published by AuthorHouse 11/30/2021

ISBN: 978-1-6655-4473-3 (sc)
ISBN: 978-1-6655-4474-0 (e)

CONTENTS

Introduction ix
Dedication xi
In Memoriam xiii
Prior Publications xv
About the Author xix

Devil's Door 1
Red, Red Rose 3
Second Class Citizen 4
Princess Patricia 6
Lidice 7
Stretch of Road 9
Dearest Daddy 10
Ode to Patricia 11
To Be 12
Apple Pie Lie 14
Hypocrisy Hill 16
Author Alley 17
Going Insane while Reading Hart Crane 19
Time's Tender Temerity 21
Nobody Here Knows Nothin' 23
Nothing Noise 24
Laptop Lucky 26
Sunday Still 27
Spanish Sunrise 28
Heartbeat of the Hills 29
The White Page 30
BM Land 33
A Toke in the Spoke 34
Dancing in the Yard 35
King of Room 23 36
Computer Crashing 37

Ga Ga Girl 39

Silhouette of Snoring. 40

Amiss Alley 41

Courtyard Catastrophe 42

South Dakota 44

This Sane Circus 45

Day After Day. 48

Center Certain 50

Monday in the Yard 52

Fly on the Wall 53

Soul of Sound 55

Hallway Howling 57

Hot Spot. 59

Roasted Roomie 61

Tears for Lear 63

Strangers Side by Side 64

Insane Lane. 67

Gloves Like Alabaster Doves 69

Solving Satan 71

The Actress. 74

Sweet Chameleon of Mine. 75

Clean Me 77

Turn Down the Volume 78

Bleeding Noise 80

Stemming the Tide 81

On My Knees When I Freeze 84

Why? 86

Another Friday Lie 87

The Man Without a Soul. 88

Glass Mass. 90

The Birth of Indifference. 92

The Actor. 93

Another Midnight. 94

No One is Listening 95

Crying on 1,001 Shoulders 96

Deacon Dawn. 98

The Return 100

Speaking to the Sky. 103

Moment by Moment. 104

Last Poem in this Notebook. 106

Click of the Pen 107

Selling Stars 108

I Create 109

Intruders in the Sky. 110

Medicine Ball Mall 112

Getting Out 114

Innosense 115

Bus Fuss 117

Beyond Expression 119

God Garage 120

Inferno Alley 122

Almost Hell 123

Blowing Up the Bridge 124

Black with a Little Brown 125

Ear Ache. 126

Portrait of a Classic Beauty 127

Patricia with a P 128

Underbelly 129

Stealing the Light 131

New York Dreaming. 132

The Lion and the Bear. 134

Sittin' in the Hallway in My Black Wheelchair. 135

Up and Down on the Nursing Home Rollercoaster 137

Beelzebub's Bank 140

In this Poet's Nightmare 142

On the Left. 143

The Way You Move 144

My Friend the Phone. 145

Twilight 146

Skin Versus Tin. 147

Making the Best of It 149

Daddy, Oh, Daddy 151

Gurney Grab. 152

Five Times a Week 154

Why Fight It? 155

5:55 AM. 156

A Thousand Winding Boulevards Leading to the Death of Your Pain 157

Frenzied Friday. 158

Another 40 Feet 159

Book Summary. 161

INTRODUCTION

This is Radomir Vojtech Luza's 35th book (31st collection of poetry).

This is his heartful and powerful muse NURSING HOME BLUES.

His poems are painful, darkly humored, joyful cries to the Skies!

Here at Grand Valley Healthcare Center in Van Nuys CA, there is Luza's pungent "Devil's Door" The iron behemoth/never lets me out. There is no snapping out/Of this zone. But firing a bullet/into the round bone. And there is the concise brilliance of his cruel, sweetly deeply touching stunner "Day After Day". The golden gun/Above the stars. At this old age home/Next to Mars Day after day/ Like window upon window/Life breaks on the nearest reef. Begging the universe/To set us free/We are monsters sipping tea. Gargoyles on/ Momma's knee.

From his electric bed, Luza ponders others' plights and slights. In "Intruders in the Sky" Why spend on roof when/Labor is understaffed and underpaid? Maybe sheen and green are more important than/A potent, pliable and powerful scene on the lean Here at Grand Valley nursing home obscene. In the funny conundrum "Stealing the Light" They're taking my roommate Walter's call light again. The Polish Pegasus has a right to the call light no matter what.

King of Room 23, Luza meditates on his Beauty Queen Patricia, also his beloved fiance. The supple and sumptuous stanzas of "Red, Red Rose" Your Sistine chapel eyes/Frozen butterflies/ Rainbow sighs The way you sashay and sway/Like an antelope at the dusk of day The way you bend at the hip/Raining grace from both lips. Your feet nimble as/This ball of blue. Sprinting through any zoo or/Atomic blast on cue. And a tender gem "Patricia with a P" Your thin shoulders/To rest my large head on. Those slim arms holding/Me round even though I/Do not make a sound.

Luza's archipelago of poverty and pain is rescued by metaphors and similes "Skin Versus Tin." "The White Page" I love myself when I write/I am a beacon with bite.

Catch the glow and flow of the last poem "Another 40 Feet" Radomir Vojtech Luza's true grit.

Sigrid Bergie Feliciano
09/15/2021

DEDICATION

This, my 35th book, is dedicated to my parents, Radomir Vaclav Luza and Libuse Luza who soared together for 52 years until my mother succumbed to ovarian cancer at 72 in 2001 and my father died a natural death of lung failure at 87 in 2009. They flew until they could fly no more. Until their wings were obliterated like asphalt streets and their dreams like porcelain porcupines.

IN MEMORIAM

My mother's mother slit her wrists and committed suicide in a white ceramic bathtub in Czechoslovakia at the age of 72 in 1973 living behind the iron curtain during the height of the Cold War. My aunt Blanka had to clean-up the blood and magenta-colored water.

My grandmother was a singer, pianist and music teacher suffering a deep depression because of the lack of freedom and liberty she felt living according to Soviet rule.

My grandmother's grizzly death underscored the brutal, inhumane and cruel Soviet system of Communist rule that offered Eastern Bloc citizens residing behind the Berlin Wall no freedom of religion, speech, art or expression and continues today in Russia, China, Cuba and North Korea, among other countries.

My grandmother was an incredibly special lady who always led the way as the family matriarch during and after WWII. Her death only underlines the horrors, mistruths and mind control that the Russian government perpetrates on a daily basis.

Their imprisonment and torture, if not murder, of political prisoners, opposition leaders, rivals and rebels is a time worn practice that has lasted well over eight decades.

God bless love, peace, kindness, art and the United States of America!!!!

PRIOR PUBLICATIONS

THE HARAHAN JOURNAL – Collection of Poetry
Dinstuhl Publishing (New Orleans, LA)

THIS N' THAT – Collection of Prose
Dinstuhl

PORCH LIGHT BLUES – Collection of Poetry
BT Publishing (Oakland, CA) Beverly Tilghman

BROKEN HEADLIGHTS – Collection of Poetry
Pigling Bland Press (Langhorne, PA)

AIRPORTS AND RAILROADS – Collection of Prose
Pigling Bland

TACKS AND ROOT BEER – Short Collection of Prose and Poetry
Ron Swegman Publishing (Philadelphia, PA)

A PRAYER FOR MONICA – Collection of Love Poetry
Pigling Bland

SHOES IN A MAGAZINE – Collection of Older Poetry
Pigling Bland

DIVA DANDRUFF – Personal Essays
Author House (Bloomington, IN)

BLUE SKY SCHOOL – Collection of Children's Poetry
Author House

SCOLIOSIS OF RAIN – Collection of Poetry
Author House

48 ON THE FLOOR – Self-Published Manuscript of 48 Poems
(Jersey City, NJ)

EVERYTHING BUT…–Self-Published Manuscript of Prose
(Jersey City, NJ)

STAGE SCRIBBLINGS – Collection of Theatre Reviews
Aurorean Music Weekly (Northern and Central NJ and NYC) (Jersey City, NJ)

STARVING SWALLOWS – Collection of Poetry
Publish America (Baltimore, MD)

TO THE NINES – Poetry Collection (Luza and Don Kingfisher Campbell)
Campbell published it through his small press (Alhambra, CA)

DAMAGED GOODS – Collection of Poetry
Dancing Sprite Publications (Radman Productions) (North Hollywood, CA)

PERSONAL POEMS – Collection of Family Poems
Poets on Site (Pasadena, CA)

MORE PERSONAL POEMS – Collection of Family Poems
Poets on Site

THE LAST COLLECTION – Collection of Poetry
Publish America

THE FOURTH NUTHOUSE IN SEPTEMBER – Collection of Short Poetry
Publish America

ROPE: Two poems
Marymark Press

CAFÉ LATTE TAPES – Collection of poetry
Publish America

NEW YORK NADIR – Collection of Poetry
AuthorHouse

EROS OF ANGELS – Collection of Poetry and Prose
AuthorHouse

WINDY CITY SONGS – Collection of Poetry
Red Doubloon Publishing (Radman Productions)

TALE OF TWO TOWNS – Collection of Poetry
Red Doubloon

CLIFFS, CALM AND COYOTES – Collection of Poetry
Red Doubloon

SIDEWALKS AND STREET CORNERS-Collection of Poetry
Christian Faith Publishing
(Meadville, PA)

MENTAL MALL-A Collection of Poetry
Four Feathers Press
(Pasadena, CA)

LOSING ME: POEMS FROM BED 23C- A Collection of Poetry
Spectrum Publishing (Pasadena, CA)

COPPER CARNATION – A Collection of Poetry
AuthorHouse

ONYX ROSE - A Collection of Poetry
Christian Faith Publishing

ABOUT THE AUTHOR

Radomir Vojtech Luza was born in Vienna, Austria in 1963 to prominent Czech parents. His sister Sabrina is fourteen-and-a-half-months younger.

The veteran SAG/AFTRA/AEA union actor, stand-up comedian, improvisational performer, host, creative non-fiction and fiction writer and disc jockey has been the poet laureate of North Hollywood, CA since 2012.

The Pushcart Prize Nominee (2012) is the author of 35 books (31 collections of poetry). This Summer he has published: LOSING ME: POEMS FROM BED 23C put-out by Spectrum Publishing in Pasadena, CA and winner of the 2021 San Gabriel Valley Poetry Festival Book Award; COPPER CARNATION, a poetry collection from AuthorHouse in Bloomington, IN and ONYX ROSE, a collection of poetry and prose published by Christian Faith Publishing in Meadville, PA.

The theatre, film and book critic (atthetheatrewithRadomirLuza.com) wonders why if he can write, record, publish and introduce four books and two powerful syndicated radio interviews in a place like Grand Valley Healthcare Center, the nursing home in Van Nuys, CA where he has spent over a year, why other artists in better environments cannot construct more creative lenses with which to view their futures.

The Tulane University and Jesuit High School graduate (New Orleans, LA) is also the winner of the Irwin Award for "Most Creative Collection of Poetry" (Book Publicists of Southern California) for EROS OF ANGELS (2016), his 400-page magnum opus.

The longtime sportswriter and freelance journalist has had poems published in over 75 literary journals, anthologies, websites and other media.

The Catholic of nearly 50 years has had his poetry featured over 110 times nationwide. The 1983 New Orleans Catholic Youth Organization Man of the Year third-place finisher has curated, organized and hosted over 15 reading series across the country in places such as New York, NY; Jersey City, NJ; Hoboken, NJ; Fort Walton Beach, FL and Los Angeles, CA.

The Topps trading card and Fanatics sports apparel collector is the editor and publisher of the literary journal, VOICES IN THE LIBRARY, published by Red Doubloon Publishing, the literary arm of Radman Productions.

DEVIL'S DOOR

Walking through the crimson gate
Here at Grand Valley Healthcare Center
In Van Nuys, CA

I do not my spirit elevate
Only lose my bearing
This late on the date

The iron behemoth
Never lets me out

As I scratch my fever with
A freight train of doubt

I gallop into my own hell
Like a genie his personal wishing well

I cannot eat or sleep
Move or groove

There is no snapping out
Of this zone

But firing a bullet
Into the round bone

Radomir luza
In Bed 3

Patricia Murphy
Oct. 14, 2021

04/15/21

RED, RED ROSE

In the moments between
Lift-off and flight
I meditate on you

Your Sistine chapel eyes
Frozen butterflies
Rainbow sighs

The way you sashay and sway
Like an antelope at the dusk of day

Your sense of humor light
But prepared for a heavyweight fight

The way you bend at the hip
Raining grace from both lips

The curve of your chest
Breasts pulling
Back pushing

I love you now and forever
Your hands soft as dew

Your feet nimble as
This ball of blue

Sprinting through any zoo or
Atomic bomb blast on cue

02/27/21

SECOND CLASS CITIZEN

(FOR THE AFRICAN AMERICAN RACE)

The police
In their brutal unknowing

Politicians
In their desperate selfishness

Corporations
In their elite arrogance

Academy Awards and Golden Globes for their
Redundant ignorance

Society in its
Racist underbelly

I am a man
Not a dog

I eat and drink
The same air as you

My skin color is
Your skin color

My children mix
With your children

My God is the same
As your God

In this crimson rhapsody
Of an existence

I am your
Brother and sister

Friend and neighbor
Doctor and teacher

Turn your head and
I am there

For better
Or worse

As rainbow
Or curse

In a throne
Or hearse

I am human like you
Jesus or Judas

02/27/21

PRINCESS PATRICIA

Yesterday through the sliding glass doors at
The neurologist's office

At Kaiser Permanente Healthcare Center in the
Soul of old Los Angeles

On an afternoon away from Grand Valley Healthcare Center
In Van Nuys, CA

You shone like the sky
Crocheted with the sun
Knitted with the dawn

Never has your nimble heart been truer
Green apple eyes freer

Your Mother Mary marching to a different beat
Sobbing on my shoulder like a long lost daughter

I relax in my gurney
Allowing the pain and doubt
Not to rule me out

03/02/21

LIDICE

When looking back on
My native country's history at

Grand Valley Healthcare Center
In Van Nuys, CA

One incident is a
Bloody sea

Small town in Czechoslovakia
During WWII

Men, women and children
lying low

Slaughtered by the Nazis
Row by row

In the early morning
One by one

As they had
No place to go

Not a human sound left
In this village bereft
Burned to death

German soldiers
Celebrating with
Czech girls and beer

The next day
On this island of gray

Black boots on the ground
Swastikas found
Arms in the air

In their eyes
A trembling tear

God weeping harder
Than King Lear

02/26/21

STRETCH OF ROAD

Leading back to me
A heart longing to be free
Not going through anyone else

Lined by magenta meadows
Crimson carnations

Feeding on crisp linen
Pregnant vacations

My life doubles
As a department store

Mannequins at the bloody front door
Dinner on the sunlit floor
Dungeons at the mighty fore

Sprinting through fields of bronze
Boulevards made of bonds

This road has skid marks and ice
Police and jungles twice
Smelling of burnt rice

06/16/21

DEAREST DADDY

From the candid conversations
To the misty revelations

I remember here at Grand Valley Healthcare Center
In Van Nuys, CA when I dare delve into the past

Your Czech accent sophisticated, sincere and witty
A most charming ditty

The WWII resistance fighter
Son of a five star army general

Choosing duty over happiness
Work not amusement

Daddy you stunned everyone
With your intellectual gun

Author of eight books
Full professor at Tulane University

Discipline and structure
Enough for three

You gave to country
Until you could no longer be

My dearest father now I see
Why I was so lucky that
You allowed me to be free

Your love the key
To my steady knee

02/08/21

ODE TO PATRICIA

The way you walk
Soft and light
Like a swan at night

At this old age home
Where never is unknown

Dancing on floors of glass and grass
Feet firing like a civil war fight

My L.A. girl
Hair fine as a thread

Skin brighter than red
Oh, Patricia
Your voice
Clear as a gun

Naked past nearer than numb
Once upon a time
Your lump sum

Dragging the arts
Under the light

Performing your
Impossible fight

Long on might
Vision not sight

Please forgive me as I from your
Abundant cornucopia bite

04/07/21

TO BE

I am
I live
And give

Here at Grand Valley Healthcare Center
In Van Nuys, CA

Play and spay
Get gray and lay

Breathe to seethe
To order steak in the wake

To love and hate like a human grate
This cobalt orb
Lost in violence and war

Pestilence galore
Greed and fourscore

Advancing to serve
And forgive

Like a satin doll
Sitting in the mall

Shattering my nerves
In the rusty suburbs

Only to learn to pray
On a pockmarked Sunday

Through the door of
The tragedy store

Where fear and doubt
Sell for 10 cents
Never more

03/11/21
APPLE PIE LIE

Here at Grand Valley Healthcare Center
In Van Nuys, CA

The sick are smarter
Than the healthy

Not begging for
Double shifts

Or diplomatically
Whispering mistruths
Behind friends' backs

Lying in bed
Tending to their heads

Like shrinks they link behavior
To a Margarita drink

Botony the day
As Jesus swims their way

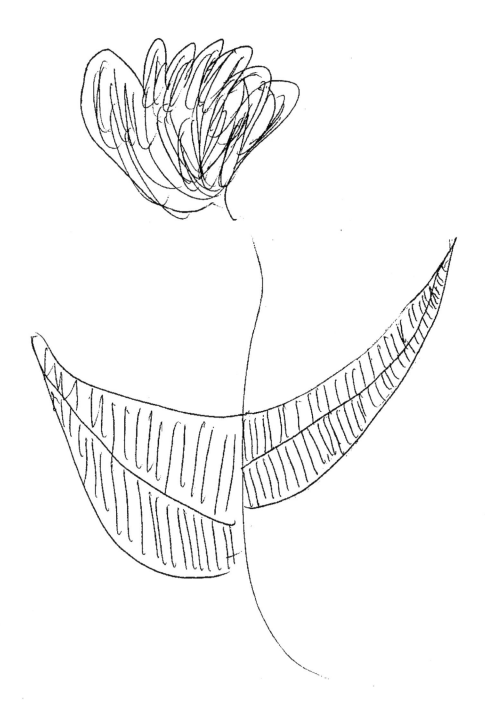

Patricia Murphy
10-7-2021

04/07/21

HYPOCRISY HILL

We multiply to divide
Add to subtract

Building skyscrapers that touch Mars
While forgetting homeless veterans
Living in cars

Tomorrow is always the answer we get
From politicians and lawyers

When today would much rather bend
For money has no soul
Only developers it likes to control

And the poor and mentally ill
It patrols

AUTHOR ALLEY

I am an author who knows not
The galaxy of this universe

Writing for self-help
Biography, food
Or some rich computer dude

Where is the substance
The very obstinance
And difference

Metaphors and mania
Raining like
Booklore and
Full whores

I miss the vision
And mission

Similes and syntax
Planets and magnets

Meadows and magnolias
Not green and bestseller sheen

The superficial
And material

I want to rhyme
For my dime

Like Shakespeare built
His bridge to God

Hemingway and Plath
Their path to another math

GOING INSANE WHILE READING HART CRANE

The bed bugs bite
Termites alight
Roaches take flight

Here at Grand Valley Healthcare Center
In Van Nuys, CA

Walking in the rain
In my own lane

I still need a Great Dane
To fight my bane

Oh, Mr. Crane
The imagery is perfect

But timing
A certain misdirect

I sit on Mars
With your complex stars

Do not understand
A word you pray

As I step away from
The page it is
Madness I cage

Soon I find myself
In the same waters you did

Except I swim for the shore
Not sink like a door

06/05/21

TIME'S TENDER TEMERITY

Grass growing
Ocean water flowing
Children knowing

Minutes replacing hours
Bumping into days
Like prison stays

Here at Grand Valley Healthcare Center
In Van Nuys, CA

Science and spirituality
On the same plane
Co-existing like a freight train

Wrinkles coming
Death at the door
Tombs once more

Please don't stare at the orange yellow sun
For it will blind you numb

Look into my transparent two
And get a clue

Time is neither here nor there
But a blink and stare
From the rare

Gamma rays and meteors
Like hibernating bears

Years but crimson butterflies
Turning into centuries

In a snap of light
Bite of sight
Mound of sound

Please God
Do not make
This blue marble
Too round

Or it will bark like a hound
End up in a police pound

Infinity bound
This grammar
But makes me stammer

For it is sturdier
Than Thor's hammer

NOBODY HERE KNOWS NOTHIN'

They walk around in uniforms and scrubs
Here at Grand Valley Healthcare Center
In Van Nuys, CA
Pretending to know it all

Never awaiting
The Fall

Unleashing a stall
Unbuckling us all

The worried and weary
Lying in electric beds
Stuffed like turkeys with meds

By nurses and doctors
Thinking they know more

CNA's overcompensating for
Geographical and language insecurities

Heads full of lead
Meds colored red

Jed fed the company line
Till he's dead

06/06/21

NOTHING NOISE

The old man watching television
All day, every day
In Bed 23A

Here at Grand Valley Healthcare Center
In Van Nuys, CA

At night
The Polish financial advisor
Advises the small screen

Absolutely nowhere as he falls asleep to
The loud noise coming from
The bingo box

Oh, grandfather dear
Get a sneer
And a life
As you disappear into the river of doubt
Under the freeway of gout

Your existence like the choice of channels
Never knowing
Forever bowing

Always sewing into
The fabric of not glowing

Diagonal to me
Please for once
Make up your mind

Forensic Files or King of Queens
Daytona auto racing or
NBA playoffs on TNT

Space or grace

LAPTOP LUCKY

Sitting on the mobile table before me
Here at Grand Valley Healthcare Center
In Van Nuys, CA

It's all iron and plastic
The vision coming before the decision

Why ahead of pie
Even Tinker Bell sighs
On the way to avoiding lies

I am fortunate to be busy
And have a purpose
A how and where

An intensity I share with technology
To rescue me

A fairy leaving the harbor
A metal and screen breath machine
Giving hope and happiness

The answer before the question
Result ahead of problem

Laptop, oh, laptop
You make me cry

You catapult me
Way up high

06/06/21

SUNDAY STILL

On the seventh day
We rest here at Grand Valley Healthcare Center
In Van Nuys, CA

Time hits an iron wall sublime
Light seeps and strains through the
Wooden blinds in Room 23

Like water through active minds
Sound into midday grinds

I am invisible
I am transparent
I am forever

On a Sunday eve
I never leave

Watching the sky
The very high
I sob like a trembling thigh

Sunday, oh, Sunday
You do not die
But quietly sigh

Steal the night
For the lie
That licks the damaged eye

SPANISH SUNRISE

The day was hot
In its neon splay

Its very gamma ray hunt
For the square root of May

The light at this old age home
Belongs to those speaking Spanish

Whether from South America, Central
America or Mexico

They love America and
Fight from beneath the snow

Until their hard work equals freedom
And a run at the sun

The yellow orange sphere on their backs
From morning to midnight
Believers in the American dream bending green

06/07/21

HEARTBEAT OF THE HILLS

There flying beneath the sun
Like bullets without a gun

The children of the moon
Citizens of the stars

My favorite professional hockey team
The best squad in all of the land

That keep me going when I get sad
Here at Grand Valley Healthcare Center
In Van Nuys, CA

Will win it all this year without a beer
Wearing the best-looking gear with no fear
Or peer

Las Vegas Golden Knights
Full of right and fight
Princes of the West

Never needing rest
The arena in Sin City

Oh, what a fest
Beautifully dressed

This is no jest
But the home of the National Hockey League's best

THE WHITE PAGE

Oh, alabaster sage
Tempting pen without rage

Here at the nursing home
My bed hides your gauge

Begging, begging for the
Sweetness of the stage

Mother, you remind me
Of the coward's cage
How to walk away and be strong

Father, you never did anything wrong
So show me your song and gong

And I will ink this sheet
This magnificent beat

With my written words
Of poetry and verse

Forward they march
Souls never full of starch
Constructing a platinum arch

Time demanding more
At the golden store

Opening the valley door
With papyrus made for four

I love myself when I write
I am beacon with bite

Train wreck on sight
Jambox June flying a spoken word kite

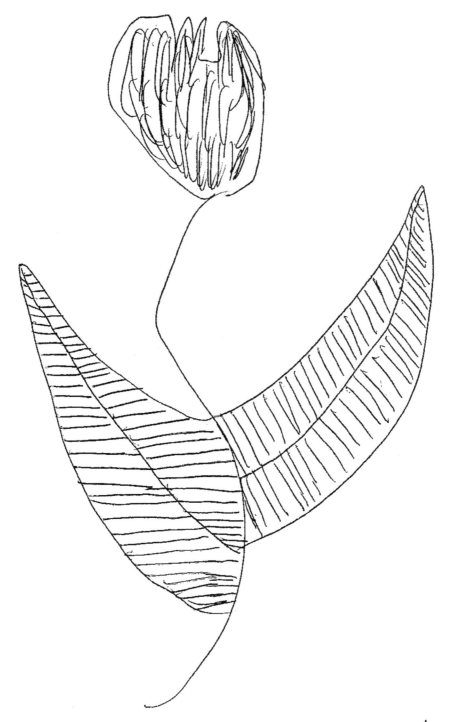

Patricia Murphy
10-7-2021

06/07/21

BM LAND

Bowel movement,
Oh, bowel movement

In this nursing home of feces

Every 15 minutes
You invade my back door

Offer not to score
Like a dilapidated whore

The pain down below often taking its toll
Later on

No writing poetry
Penning verse
When I feel it in reverse

Get the plastic bag and gloves
Rip out the monster
Before it shoves

The suffering in the hole is done
It will return after lunch

In this God forsaken jail
Where not even the mail
Has a direct snail

A TOKE IN THE SPOKE

Here in the courtyard of the
Grand Valley Healthcare Center
In Van Nuys, CA

Nurses, CNA's and RNA's
Smoke cigarettes during their breaks

The best of the best killing themselves slowly
Polluting the same bodies
They tell us to keep pristine and clean
The same lungs they help operate on

The identical vessels destroyed by nicotine and
Tobacco inhalation

Oh, hypocrisy thy name is human
Thy game anxiety and fear
For those telling us to be relaxed
Are anything but themselves

Oh, human nature
Thy name is pain

Thy refrain bane
Thy calling card inane
For to do what one knows is harmful

A cue for lack of pew
Old hue on view at the zoo

06/08/21

DANCING IN THE YARD

I dance in the courtyard of this
Nursing prison
Like I count stars in the midnight sky

As if it was a fantasy
A very fairytale
A raspberry strawberry
Fondue of the mind

I dance to remember
I dance to forget

The moments easing in and out
Of my life like a tin band

I dance to sweat
I dance to let

I boogie to allow
The demons to go

Slow madness to sanity to grow
Altruism to flow
Tears down my copper cheeks

06/08/21

KING OF ROOM 23

I sit in my electric bed
Watching the other two heads taking meds

At Grand Valley Healthcare Center
In Van Nuys, CA

And I am emperor of the room
King of the space
Don't need no mace

Looking into the hallway
Like a neon gamma ray

Saying hello to my friends
As if time never ends

Both roommates assessing me
Taking cues from my
Actions, words and threes

I am king bee
Napoleon
Alexander the Great

Sitting in power
Lying like a flower
Watching tv for an hour

God granting me
My own tower

06/09/21

COMPUTER CRASHING

When the ceiling falls
Good luck stalls
Walls close in like broken malls

In this beat-up nursing home
I go to the laptop for relief

Finding Fanatics.com
And emptying just about all that belongs

Buying sports apparel
From the four major
American sports leagues

And their brethren is
A second life

Bringing peace enough
For a family of four
Once they close the door

Sports is my first love
And I need to represent
So my stay here is far from heaven sent

Blaming my fiance for sticking me here
I harbor too many resentments to
Make my exit clear

A click here and there
Helps me find confidence and faith

A tranquility only angels and saints possess
And a small screen
In this city of less
Allowing me to assess

06/09/21

GA GA GIRL

When I'm sad or down
These vanilla walls start closing in

I gaze into the busy hallway
Here at Grand Valley Healthcare Center
In Van Nuys, CA

At the gorgeous girls peopling this rusty tube
Whether staring at top or bottom
The ladies help me feed

Ambushed dreams and forbidden scenes
I never told my family about feeling like a lout

I stand forever stout
Fighting a bout I can never win

On this Archipelago of
Love and sin

Whiskey and gin
Friends and kin

Poetry and Anais Nin
Pain from a sharp pin

The trials of actor Anthony Quinn
Listening to this band of tin
When I win

06/09/21
SILHOUETTE OF SNORING

If you can count on one thing
In room 23 of the Grand Valley Healthcare Center
In Van Nuys, CA

It is the slumbering of eons
The very knitting of voices
Crocheting of lungs

Stillness of centuries
Focus of frogs

For we three sleep like lions
Walk like Mayans
Live like the marriage of God and science

06/11/21

AMISS ALLEY

This valley of brutality
Army of pain

Does not stop
Unmaking sense

Tongues wagging
CNA's bragging

Here at the nursing home in Van Nuys, CA
Nothing works
Not my right arm
Right leg
Or lower left back

I am a cripple
Caged like a pierced nipple

Landmines galore
At this sad store
Containing only more

Anything can go wrong
At anytime

Setting recovery back
Three months

I want out without fighting
A bloody bout
With no galloping doubt

06/12/21

COURTYARD CATASTROPHE

Sitting in the cement yard
For the first time

In a white and red
Nike Just Do It t-shirt

From Social Services'
Stockpile of clothes

Listening to Bob Seger's Hollywood Nights
On Norman's smartphone

Here at Grand Valley Healthcare Center
In Van Nuys, CA

Bronze button
Shining Shasta

Burning a hole
Through my extra large wheelchair

Three dollar green trees in the distance
Pockmarking the ocean blue sky

No clouds
No doubts

No trembling hands
Or shaking thighs

This is my crimson rhapsody
Pristine variety
Orange yellow tragedy

I could be here forever
Sitting and swaying
In the midday warmth

While the world passes me by
And my life is never more dry

If certainly not high
In this magenta truth turned lie

06/12/21

SOUTH DAKOTA

You never really belonged here
Lauren Scott

A ghost flittering against
The Los Angeles sky

On the internet at the nursing home
I learned with a sigh

A flamingo pink
And don't ask why

Flashing tits at
The George Floyd wall

Instagram and the
Sudden harang

Dead at 27 in the motorhome
In which you weighed a gram

Now no more abuse, drugs, alcohol
Or strange men to color your zen

Just one more homeless body
Named Dakota Skye

Forgotten as soon as it dries
Another Hollywood lie

06/12/21

THIS SANE CIRCUS

Fifth crazy patient in same bed in Room 23
Here at Grand Valley Healthcare Center
In Van Nuys, CA

Nurse, nurse
Pressing call light to no response
When someone comes

Tv on high
Low
High again

Nurse comes
Nurse, nurse

I cannot think
Barely Blink
Of urine and sweat stink

I need a cola drink
And a good shrink

He is deaf for to me
He does not listen
Only his ego cushion

Nurse, nurse
Of a different world

Built on a Polish swirl
Unamerican curl

I am about to hurl
In this facility cold
As an Atlantic pearl

The clowns came
But they looked the same

Throwing his medicine
Down the drain

Just to have
Someone to blame

Inside their dumb and
Deadly game

Patricia Murphy
10-7-2021

06/13/21
DAY AFTER DAY

The golden gun
Above the stars

At this old age home
Next to Mars

Lingers warmly
In our cars

Day upon day
We do not know what
Will come our way

So we pray
But even God does not
Always get us to May

24 hours with which we play
Seven times in a quadruple sway

Are we in charge or is
Something else at large

Day after day
Like window upon window
Life breaks on the nearest reef

Begging the universe
To set us free
We are monsters sipping tea

Gargoyles on
Momma's knee

Day after day
What we see
Is different from you and me

06/14/21

CENTER CERTAIN

I am neither left nor right
Blue or red
White nor black

Not politically dead
Here at Grand Valley Healthcare Center
In Van Nuys, CA

I am gray
As the overcast day

I love Israel
And support a permanent stay with Hamas

I gaze into the mirror lately
And all I see is a never ending fuss about me

Complete with complexes and insecurities
To fill the Red Sea

But I move on as I must
As I will

As God wants me to do
And Beelzebub does not
As the Jewish state does

As my search for the perfect poem continues
So does the need for a third party

And a political system based on
Need not greed

A love of national seed
I am not nervous when I forget service

For I know it is in my DNA
Like a cloudy May

MONDAY IN THE YARD

Sitting in the courtyard
Near the glass door

At the Grand Valley Healthcare Center
In Van Nuys, CA
Sky bluer than a Pepsi-Cola can

Clouds invisible
Heat visible
Words indivisible

My youth passing before me
My life slipping behind me

Time stealing moments as they pass
Afternoon bright as midnight mass

Beaming like a laser
Powerful as a taser
Lost like a trailblazer

06/16/21

FLY ON THE WALL

Drowning in L.A. spit
We are knights of shit

Dry as mother earth
Loud as a baby's birth

The homeless
Living on freeway exits
Under interstate overpasses

Venice Beach in crisis
We need beautiful Isis

Mayor yacking this
After yacking that

Only interested in reelection
And reaffirmation

While the citizens bleed
From need

Scarred from too many cars
This city of devils
This town of horizontal bevels

Gargoyles eating May
Sucking day

Surf disappearing behind cloud of gray
Long lost in blue jays and seagulls

Now hours away from a dagger in the ground
A loud bray in the hay

Stinking of urine and sweat
L.A. you take my big ugly bet

06/17/21

SOUL OF SOUND

The hallway hounds
Never making a sound

At Grand Valley Healthcare Center
In Van Nuys, CA

Looking for grit
In some Shakespeare wit

Damming our mouths
With alabaster clouds

Who can we be but
Who we were at birth

Shying away from
Our very earth

Like strangers meeting
At an intimate hearth

Giving away our
Spiritual girth

Landing on the
Next planet

Maybe the sun will
Grill the granite

Until we, the sinners,
Locate mirth

On Mars'
Weakened worth

06/17/21

HALLWAY HOWLING

The screams and dreams
Of every room
Under the asphalt seam

Like the yelling and ego swelling
Of the mighty hordes

Here at Grand Valley Healthcare Center
In Van Nuys, CA

If not a nurse
Then a curse

If a cleaning
Then a streaming

Always wanting this or that
A miss or a hat

Time working its own game
In its loose frame

I came but the hours were lame
So I left to escape this theft

Over there in the green zone
Where bones come home to die
I needed a loan
Of freedom and stone

But all I got was another
Shot in the dark

Like a spark with
Nowhere to bark

A lark with its own
Brand of bark

06/18/21

HOT SPOT

Sweat pouring off my supple wrists
Burning my old cysts
Like Southern grits

Maybe it's just the Summer
Here at Grand Valley Healthcare Center
In Van Nuys, CA

Or global warning
Is no hoax

Heat bending glass
Between two Cokes

Room 23 a deathtrap
For us three

As we survive a week
Of sunny therapy

Oh, sixth month,
Break not so hard
On this orb of the bard

Be still
Do not kill

Or we will to
July cling

Like a bride burning her ring
A rapper his bling

A young Judy Garland
A song to sing

06/18/21

ROASTED ROOMIE

Lying in bed
Sad and sick

Fed from a tube
Hanging on a steel rod

Plastic bottle
With brown food
Your tude

But you lie on your back
Not moving or grooving

Merely a body
Still and unfulfilled

Not giving
Or living

Merely being and
Not seeing

Unhealthy not
Fine or good

There is no
Climbing the fence

Bring him to a hospital
To see what is wrong

It is the oppressive heat
On the seat

The sweltering humidity
Biting captivity

Wet gown on you
Skin a reddish hue

Tongue never wagging
Body sagging

Open the gates to hell
So this Polish man can ring the bell
And show us where he fell

Please tell him how to jell
Before another coughing spell
Spinning him to a warmer cell

Roommate don't be so gloomy
Find the path to Rumi

06/20/21
TEARS FOR LEAR

At least once–a–day
For over six months

Here at Grand Valley Healthcare Center
In Van Nuys, CA

Moss drops from
An oak tree

Shooting stars
Pay a fee

Meteors are
Never free

Freight trains end up
Like Robert E. Lee

Torpedoes dive to
The sunken sea

Momma please don't tell them
All about me

For then they would know the
Work of this Queen Bee

All death and no knee

STRANGERS SIDE BY SIDE

Sliding down this boulevard of dreams
At Grand Valley Healthcare Center
Here in Van Nuys, CA

That seem so extreme
You sleeping in the bed
Diagonal to mine

And I am with you
Night and day

But who are you?
Are you who you say you are?

Or will the rain fall
For a new bane?

I look through you
But do not know you

Conquering the Shastas of my existence
Like a leopard with lice

All grace
But no spice

I cannot you understand
For we are all one-man bands

Pretending to be
Symphonies

Operas of
Disaster

Philharmonics
Of pain

Playgrounds of
Pornography

I may hold
Your hand

Take a
Courageous stand

But never on
Mars land

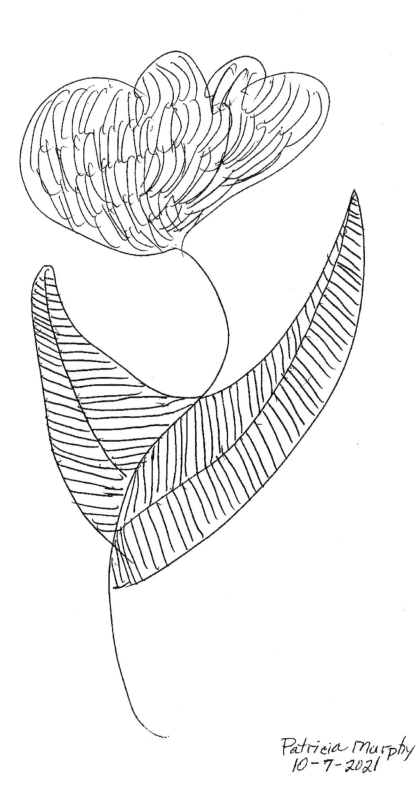

Patricia Murphy
10-7-2021

06/20/21

INSANE LANE

No matter where I look at
Grand Valley Healthcare Center
In Van Nuys, CA

Crazy people invading the sane
Selfish and loud
Never proud

Offering no more
Than what they can

Life is a peacock fan
Urinal ban

Unicorn slam
Hollywood ram

The insane in beds
Taking meds
With white-haired heads

In wheelchairs
In the courtyard

Stating their cases
To no one in particular

While we turn our heads
In glee

On this
Island decree

Knowing that we all will be
Free eventually

They sit in their dirty socks
And masturbate

While we stay fit in our mocks
And hesitate

06/20/21

GLOVES LIKE ALABASTER DOVES

All over the skilled nursing facility
Gloves come in huge cartons
Like pearls in oceans

But these special gloves
Are ripped-out of small boxes and worn by

Nurses, doctors and CNA's before
The big moment

Medical grade vinyl
Powder free exam gloves
To the rescue

No one has the courage
To examine the rectum
Barehanded

Sometimes they double
The synthetic sensors

But always servants to
Safety and security

No one dares going
Ungloved

Like dogs sniffing love
And buying a house
On the neighbor's roof above

Strangers donning plastic mittens
To clean me

I want skin
Not tin

SOLVING SATAN

We drink gin
Then grin
Commit sin

All the while disgracing the devil
When we should be looking in the
Mirror and changing our ways

We rape, pillage, plunder and molest
Then want to go home and
Watch The Hollywood Squares

We cheat on out fiances and mates
Then want a roundtrip ticket
To our fate

Oh, lord when we get to the Pearly Gates
What will you say?

You won't blame the devil
But gaze into our headlights

And open our many
Slights and fights

Only to send us to purgatory
Where we spend eternity
Floating between heaven and hell

Ringing Beelzebub's bell
When we should be getting up from
Where we fell

Having only our passion and voice to sell
Prison of our own making to dwell

Curtain of Blood

When considering my family history here at
The nursing home

If red was the color of the USSR
So it was the color of the ceramic white tub
My grandmother took her last breath in

As any true artist would looking for idealism and love
And finding it crushed by Soviet ranks and tanks

And a political agenda that called for no
Freedom of religion, speech or artistic expression

Oppression at its worst
The Soviet Union at its most cursed

My mother's mother slit her wrist that night
At 72 in 1973 and died

A rose slowly fading under the midday sun
Like a turquoise sky marred by a gray gun

My aunt, her daughter, cleaning the vanilla vase
Joining the ill-fated club with one rub

The corpse an unexplainable stain on
One country's inexhaustible claim of a
Positive and glorious aim

In this world of platinum corroded by
Rusty aluminum

THE ACTRESS

When thinking about my life here at
The old age home

My mother wanted nothing more than a
Shakespeare score
A Sophocles or Aeschylus more

She was Antigone in tragic lore
At the Czech National Conservatory
That was a second home

Anything was possible and she
Living proof

Until Adolph Hitler and his black storm
Proved that notion laughable

The Blitzkrieg ended her beginning
Like stomping boots and swastika suits
Began her end

Escaping Nazism and the Communism
That followed scarred the Edelweiss in her soul

But not the Fuhrer in the hole

Where she went to die at 72
The same age as her mother

A coincidence that was
Not just another

SWEET CHAMELEON OF MINE

Here at the nursing facility
Pondering the past

When children
Less different we
Could not have been

Sabrina my younger sister
The second coming of the first
But without most of the blister

In college
My punk did not meet
Your sorority spunk

And we were never
The same

In this pockmarked world
You played a different game

One without a name
With a cardboard frame
And the coldest same

Ice queen, oh,
Ice queen

Why are you so mean?
Freezing tulips on Amsterdam's green

Your love of humanity ever so lean
Your selfishness always at full steam

You are three people in one
You have no problems
So you gave us a ton

CLEAN ME

As I sit non-transfixed in my electric bed
At Grand Valley Healthcare Center
In Van Nuys, CA

The Summer heat
Makes me feel dead

I walk the sun in
My nimble imagination

Lacking any form of
Sure transportation

On this island of
Stucco and cement

All I hear is
"Clean me now"
As the CNA's vent

I would not want a job here for
The Queen's billions
Jeff Bezos' trillions

Lifting feces from the frame
Cleaning urine just the same

These heroes just play the game
Having no one to blame
Which would not be so lame

06/24/21

TURN DOWN THE VOLUME

Whether Law and Order: SVU
NBA Western Conference Finals Game Two

The sound on your tv too loud
Here in Room 23 of Grand Valley Healthcare Center
In Van Nuys, CA

Making me, your roommate, anything but proud
In this suffix of insanity
Room of reality

I cannot sleep
Dream
Eat

Work or be neat
With the blaring noise

But roomie does not care
Only brush his hair
In this lonely lair

The idiot box
His only friend

Moving closer
To the end

Old man, remember
I am your friend
No matter the bend

Throw away the crutch
Find relevance in silence

06/24/21

BLEEDING NOISE

Absorbing the dawn
At 5:55 AM
Here at Grand Valley Healthcare Center
In Van Nuys, CA

I lay on the imaginary lawn
Longing for beauty of any kind
No longer found in Room 23
Or anywhere in humanity

I write to collect moments
Like baseball cards

Beauty like rare stamps
Red Bacchus Mardi Gras doubloons
At the ready

Valley of volatility
Peak of panic

Oh, lord
Do not take away my pen
Or the wren inspiring my zen

06/24/21

STEMMING THE TIDE

I look for any way I can stem the bay
Like a vanishing breed
I search my deed
Not my seed

I pray and pray for change
For a more beautiful world
In this sad and hungry swirl

A path to Nirvana
On a creative whirl

Leaping and laughing like a little girl
Locating God's referral

In Room 23 of this nursing home mural
Painted in depth and width

Focused in scope and color
Hope and Robert Mueller

I dive into my muse and
Turn off the fuse

The road to salvation does not go
Through anyone else but me

The fists of my nation are not
Raised at another time

Holding back the day from
The promise I pray

The tears from the
Mounting years

Patricia Murphy
10-7-2021

06/25/21
ON MY KNEES WHEN I FREEZE

When looking back on my youth
Here at Grand Valley Healthcare Center
In Van Nuys, CA

I grasp the remnants of madness
Bits and pieces of sanity

Parents who loved too much
Sister who never did

The house of horrors at
839 Roseland Parkway in Harahan, LA

A barrage of verbal abuse for over a year
Everyday on the hour
I had no power

Brought to state mental hospital
By state troopers in wrist and ankle cuffs

My, oh, my how did life suddenly get so rough?
Saying one thing
Doing another

Climbing on my knee
All three
Like vine on the sea

It all comes back to me
My talent can see
No wide open spaces
On these long and frightened faces

Very low on their spiritual graces
In these far and forbidden places

06/25/21

WHY?

Why am I still in this nursing facility?
Its iron doors
Wayward whores

Frozen floors
Empty lore

Over half a year
Without a beer

This King Lear has no fear
Of time or the sublime

He wants out
Surely and without a doubt

No nurses or CNA's populating his dreams
Like obscene seams
Pornographic daydreams

Why?
I want to cry or die
But I will keep dry and sigh

At this wooden lie
Captain Bligh on high

My, oh, my
How sly

My soul
Sahara desert dry

06/25/21
ANOTHER FRIDAY LIE

One more weekend
Here at Grand Valley Healthcare Center
In Van Nuys, CA
And I still do not walk

Waiting for my wounds to heal
Is the big deal

Now that they are solid and standard
Where is the doctor's order for true physical therapy?

But I no longer believe in this physician or the
Physical therapy staff or this God-awful
Nursing staff and their CNA's

Take them as I throw them
One lie bigger than the next

Have not seen my doctor since time began
This place ran worse than Iran

No longer hanging on the truth
But a sharp tooth and bottle of Vermouth

06/26/21

THE MAN WITHOUT A SOUL

Choices and decisions
Like voices and religions
Noises and exhibitions

Here at Grand Valley Healthcare Center
In Van Nuys, CA

I am a spiritual pauper
Accepting myself more
For who I am than who
I want to be

Gazing into the past
As much as the present

I have learned to fast
For there is no conspiracy vast

Time escaping fast
Heart up and down like mast

I no longer know how I am cast
Or if I will last

Everyone is dying
No one is trying

Where am I headed?
A planet unleaded?
Purgatory netted?

I have no soul
My body a hole
Emptiness the goal
Frenzy the mole
Slippery this pole

06/27/21

GLASS MASS

When all was wrong
The Broadway poster was right

In my dream here at Grand Valley Healthcare Center
In Van Nuys, CA

Everything was beautiful
When I was young

As I got older
It got colder

At 23 I touched the glass
Felt the green grass
Fell on my Czech ass

Theatre was church
Art the bridge
To God's search

The play my soul and goal
When in my youth it was
My front tooth

Yelling and screaming
Wanting and needing

Desiring and feeding
My Great White Way greeting

My ideals
Once true
Now threw

Resurfaced while kissing
This poster of blue
Like a well-worn cue

Facing the street
The sheet was red meat

New York, NY
You stuffed my cork

Until like
Mork

I flew
To Ork

06/30/21

THE BIRTH OF INDIFFERENCE

When children play
They are one with God

When they stop they become adults
Bullying, bragging and bristling
At the taste of boredom

You can see who they are
And why

As they grow-up ignorance follows
Jealousy grows
Pain murders sensitivity

At this nursing home
Indifference is emperor
Anxiety king
Adults do nothing but sting

06/30/21

THE ACTOR

God makes only a few like me
Drinking from the ocean as far as I can see

Climbing Mount Olympus
Understanding the genius of General Robert E. Lee

Working harder than any bumble bee
Comprehending that one times one
Equals three

Crossing highways to be free
Allowing myself the time to be

Paying no fee for eating Brie
Scraping my knee or sipping tea

Performing through the storm
To find my Zen here at Grand Valley Healthcare Center
In Van Nuys, CA

Shedding the dark and dreary pen
My karma shrieking like a wren
Or a starving hen

07/01/21

ANOTHER MIDNIGHT

Curtains brown
Devil knocking on my gown
Here at Grand Valley Healthcare Center
In Van Nuys, CA

As I reinforce the store
I am choking on suicidal thoughts

Drowning in
Shortness of breath

Will I ever be the same?
My talent remain?

Now I must believe
To plant a larger seed

Or I will spend the rest of my days
Sipping on misery

Its black teeth stained by grime
And time

Sucking on Beelzebub's slime
I scream but no one hears

I yell and
Nobody can tell

07/01/21
NO ONE IS LISTENING

I have tried against bits of sky
Cried eating hits of pie

Screaming next to unerring dreams
Yelling on top of a wishing well
And no one is there to help me

Carry me from ditch to bridge
Itch to ridge

Caterwauling under
Pieces of dawn

Universe is much too long
No helping hands
Laughing lands

Elevators full of marching bands
Not making a sound

Here at Grand Valley Healthcare Center
In Van Nuys, CA

When I am on the ground
Or drying my tears
In this world of fears

07/02/21

CRYING ON 1,001 SHOULDERS

Tears falling
Steers stalling
Buffalo calling

At Grand Valley Healthcare Center
In Van Nuys, CA

Here I am again
Sabre at my side
Sword to glide

Everyday a brand new reason
For feeling treason

Roaming with
The clouds

Flying with
The crowds

I am never myself
For I do not know
Who that is

Or why he
Is alive

Dancing in jail
Prancing without mail

Doing it all for the saltwater flowing down my cheeks
For I am too weak to see beyond the bleak

Too frightened to deaden the pain
Too misunderstood to stay out of her lane

Too terrified to hold onto the sane
Too molested to let go of the mane

Too crazy not to listen to the inane or
Stay away from goodness my bane

07/03/21
DEACON DAWN

Pockets of pink
Against bowling ball blue sky

Here at Grand Valley Healthcare Center
In Van Nuys, CA

No clouds way up high
Only perceptions of how and where

On this Saturday
Before July 4th

An uneven stare
At this pockmarked lair

The truth building
Light wielding
Sun yielding

Pure as God on the throne
Of this dome

Poised to bend
With no end
Or beginning

Trees still as sentries
Bushes and flowers like boulders

Holding back the tears
Through the rigid fears

Running through the years
Kicking back the beers

The Hollywood King Lears
Unstable deers

Killing the sky without asking why
Drinking rye behind the corner cry
Standing still like an alarm drill

07/04/21
THE RETURN

Reading in rhyme
Metered in time
Dancing on the vine

Reciting poetry at my first reading
In sixteen months

Covid-19 the brazen crime
Feeling like a giant
With a palace of dimes

My life on the move
Everything right to the Louvre

Metaphors mixed
Similes fixed

Verse thick as ham
Expression full as a ram

Art dancing
Down the boulevard
Like anything but lard

Playing the content card
In this gymnasium fit for the bard
Proved he was on guard
Salient but scarred

Here at Grand Valley Healthcare Center
In Van Nuys, CA

Flexing my poetic muscles
Like a madman in Brussels
Who like an oak rustles
With the sky tussles

And possesses the sweetest set
Of corpuscles

Patricia Murphy
10-7-2021

07/04/21

SPEAKING TO THE SKY

It is hard to blink
When love like an animal stinks

In this nursing home sublime
Dreaming of cannibals on narrow ridges

Cars careening off slim bridges
Like children breaking on a bloody raking

Steamboats turning on the Mississippi
Like lightning rods burning St. Francis of Assisi

Love long and languid
Legs soft as rain

On this conclave of bane
Diet of the mind
Relaxing purgatory's bind

As the nurse
Widows the crime

In a prison for the insane
Only madness cures the pain

As we do not see
A slap on the broken knee

07/05/21

MOMENT BY MOMENT

Time is all we have
Like sand by the ocean

A castle on a bumpy ridge
A child with a notion

Living our lives
Day by day
Hour by hour

Like a reluctant flower
Or a Mardi Gras doubloon shower

Moment by moment
Shore after shore
More by more

We discover who we are
Bit by bit
Piece by piece
Zit by zit

Uncovering what we know for
What we do not

Who we trust
For every bust

Why poetry fits each score
The word the foundation for every crown
God's message without a frown

Jesus and the pronouns
Judas and the bloody gown
Caesar and his unlit town

Me and my momentary down
Riding the apex to the universe's sound

07/05/21

LAST POEM IN THIS NOTEBOOK

As the last
It is the first

As the first
It is the last

In this notebook of verse
Crying for the reverse

There is pathos and dark humor here
Missed by those without a fear
Or lacking a poetic sneer

The beauty radiates like
A diamond under the sun

A pearl awash in the One
Mowing down preconceptions and
Lost convictions

This final ditty
Lost in this insane city

Down with the nitty and gritty
Feeling no pity
Like that criminal Gordon Liddy

Life here wonderfully giddy
Like that of Walter Mitty

In its own way very witty
Without resorting to pleasing the kiddies

07/05/21

CLICK OF THE PEN

Pen, pen
When, when
Feeding the wren, wren
With rainbow Zen, Zen

Ink black and blue
Color always true

Pen, oh, mighty pen
I feel a sharp glen
An impossible glade

But you maneuver
The most difficult
Of turns with the
Slightest of burns

Papyrus you drown
In your considerable frown

Click, click, click
Of Bic, Bic, Bic
With a wild kick, kick, kick
Of this stick, stick, stick

07/06/21

SELLING STARS

Here at Grand Valley Healthcare Center
In Van Nuys, CA

The sky falling on me
Like dreams that disagree

Trees swaying like dance partners
Without a knee

Bushes moving like
Hogs before slaughter

Meteors crashing like
King Creon's daughter

Creating my own world
Like a nimble squirrel

Fate dropping a bomb
Like the protestors in Hong Kong

Constructing the lens to my daddy's Benz
I know I was born too late

Like a poet
Without a fate

07/07/21

I CREATE

At this nursing home I discover
The sun for it has nowhere to run

The sky as it asks why
The moon shimmering in June

The trees like sentries
Protecting the gate

The seagulls like soldiers
Overlooking their bait

The oceans like rivers
Crisscrossing the grate

Sand like pebbles
Waiting for fate

Hands like horns
Crushing chord C

Sins like rats
Emerging from purgatory

INTRUDERS IN THE SKY

Asphalt like rain
Falling from pane

Electricity off
Internet not on

Tornado atop
Boots cleaning shop

Wham here
Bam there

Fixing the roof
One big spoof

In a year or more
Holes in the floor

Never done
Always on the run

This is no fun
Being under the gun

Banging like a hanging
Nooses in the air

Equipment on the flare
Pressure down there

Black pieces into
The window

Like a
Government overthrow

Singing a song
That can only go wrong

Why spend on roof when
Labor is understaffed and underpaid?

Maybe sheen and green are more important than
A potent, pliable and powerful scene on the lean

Here at Grand Valley nursing home obscene

MEDICINE BALL MALL

Every inch of pinch
A synch

Each weight and band
A pebble in the sand

Here at Grand Valley Healthcare Center
In Van Nuys, CA

This is up to me
I want to be free

Stretching me as far
As I can see

Conquering thunderstorms
In the snow

My own demons as
They go

The steeper the hurdle
The tighter the stretch

Whatever is put before me
Is soon after me

A heart the size of Everest
A soul doing its best

Physical therapy
From the chest

Anchored in
No rest

Give me all you can
I'll shock you with Zen

Right leg moving better
Than a wren

My existence
Strongly reflected

My life
Passionately enacted

GETTING OUT

No matter the administrator or paper
They throw at me

I am gone
Out the door
Quarter to four

Giving me all
The reasons I should stay

Like a pumpkin in the hey
Two old roommates in the gray

Room 23 a trap for the map
No way out

Milking my insurance
Until it makes no sense

Walking out to make me glad
Sorting out the good and bad
Making time the only fad

In this insane box of screaming and socks
Metal cage of steel and heal
Stucco hut of random mutts

Even Hal would
Be no pal

07/13/21

INNOSENSE

We strive for sense
Out of ignorance

Reason and logic
To make us feel bold

Instead all that fodder leads to
Welcome Back Kotter

Please make
No sense

There is no evidence
Or middle fence
Hence no Mike Pence

Allowing the instinct
And soul to search

For those green glades
In the perch

Letting go of thought
Here at Grand Valley Healthcare Center
In Van Nuys, CA
Must be taught
To the bought, sought and distraught

Only the absurd and not heard
Can stop the buffalo herd
Which know not the word
Coming first in God's platinum bird

Learn to peace

Sing in the cat By [chance]

No [square]

From the or the white House

Power fu Leadership

Know Harmony

the forest

Peace and Harmony

A place of

Peace of

— Dash and bolt to

Misuse of funds

Radomir Vojtechluza 10-1-2021

7/13/21
BUS FUSS

At 5AM

They entered
All five
Into their favorite dive

Sitting across from me

All hands and elbows
Retinas and tongues

I was Joe Frazier
Always moving forward

They were George Foreman
Never the same after Ali

Mornings filled with loud voices
Vivid choices

Fists flying
Dreams dying

Dawn broke
I spoke

All color and
No fear

Soon the claws were gone
It was Forest Lawn

All clear
Right here

My empty pockets spoke
Existence was no joke

Today happened again
Until I walked away
The noblest of men

An army of one
Drinking liquid sun

07/14/21

BEYOND EXPRESSION

While contemplating the current state of humanity at
Grand Valley Healthcare Center in Van Nuys, CA
It occurred that

We walk in the shadow of mountains
Lick the sky in tremendous flying machines

Hug the earth in swift racecars
Tickle the imagination with 20 foot movie screens

Nudge gray matter with thinking machines
Put 3,000 printed pages of wisdom on a hand-held device

Kill over 100 million people in two World Wars

But forget and deny the existence of the Infinite
In thought, creation, labor and action

07/14/21

GOD GARAGE

While meditating on God at Grand Valley Healthcare Center
In Van Nuys, CA it became obvious that

What was in the sky and clouds
Sight and sounds

Now exists in our pores with
The least of whores

Hearts empty
Souls barren
Being staring

Beauty is our goal
Yet there are so many holes

The Infinite is where we go to the show
The very slow mow

Climbing clearly
Falling nearly

Mixing Margarita and beer
Radiance and a sneer
Harmony and fear

Blue peaks
Alabaster weeks

Turquoise leaks
Crimson beaks

Pistachio cheeks
Cherry freaks

Riding my God beat
On this blessed freeway seat

Where love meets
Lonesome dove up above

07/15/21

INFERNO ALLEY

We jump and groove
Dance and move

All the while
Fooling and dueling
With the One above

We drink and stink
Insert heroin into our favorite link

And hope He won't notice
While we destroy and denigrate

This beautiful blue marble of May and day
Ignoring and denying more than red clay
But the souls we never weigh

07/15/21
ALMOST HELL

Hanging in there
As long as we can bear

At Grand Valley Healthcare Center
In Van Nuys, CA

Blood and guts
In this solipsistic lair

Stinking of all we speak of
But do not dare

Momma please do not so sadly stare
Poppa so madly glare

All I ask for is a cheaper fare
To Purgatory

Where we all bear
The sins of an older bunch

Who sadly grew the paranoia we so well knew
Growing on vines of a darker hue

Leaping from stages where we flow like one body
Painted in glow

07/15/21
BLOWING UP THE BRIDGE

I am tired of standing and fighting
In this nursing facility

I want to go
Whale sighting

But this planet needs
Those like me

Strong and happy
To be free

Oh, bluest of orbs
Do not misunderstand me

I would die for you
Were you not so oblique

Lift you on my shoulders
Like one large boulder

Open the door and you will see more of this
Unseemly department store
Open to visitors until 4

BLACK WITH A LITTLE BROWN

Here at Grand Valley Healthcare Center
In Van Nuys, CA

Darkness she bleeds
Love she does not feed

Fear her seed
Envy her greed

She dare not spot a miracle
For it cages her tongue

She has never had a dream
As it ages her lung

Please God do not cuff her heart
For it freezes the young

This woman needs redemption
Until it is neither verb nor noun

But unfiltered sound

07/16/21

EAR ACHE

When considering the human race at
Grand Valley Healthcare Center in Van Nuys, CA,
it appears that

We wake up at dawn to mow the lawn
Watch the colleges on Saturdays
Root for our favorite pro football teams on the seventh day

But are deaf to the cries of the starving in Africa
Because they are not in America

Refuse to listen to the homeless as they do not matter
Laugh at the retarded because we are better

Attack our gay brothers and sisters for we see a piece of themselves in us
Refusing to listen to anything different from what we believe

We slumber through mass while rationalizing organized religion
And the two party political system

Advocating for racism and the hoax of climate change
We die at dusk and find our corpses at the shore in the morning

Forgetting our hearts and souls in a soup bowl
We have forgotten how to love ourselves and our neighbors

Merely cutting through existence like dull knives
Galloping into eternity with wasted lives

PORTRAIT OF A CLASSIC BEAUTY

(Dedicated to Sona)

Oceans moving under your feet
Buildings collapsing into heat

Clouds floating near your hand
Sky falling into sand

Face as fine as the Mona Lisa
Perfect figure sculpted by land

Eyes like snow ball stands
Hair threads of fleece

Beauty with a stare
As powerful as Greece

Gaze as deep as
Simplicity leased

You are a human feast
At least

07/19/21

PATRICIA WITH A P

In these days of suicidal thoughts
Love meant not bought

I need you more than
A ship does the ocean

A plane does the sky
A car does the freeway
A train does not ask why

Your thin shoulders
To rest my large head on

Those transparent eyes
Comforting this broken soul
Like a modern hole

Those slim arms holding
Me round even though I
Do not make a sound

You with your own problems
Still finding a path to this new math

Road to the hour of power
Avenue to the bar of stars

Boulevard to the mounds of clouds

07/20/21

UNDERBELLY

While thinking about Los Angeles at the nursing home
The monster's mouth going South

Teeth like spikes
Dining on our souls
Devouring our goals

Why can we not figure it out?
The barrier between artist and lout

Dipping my feet into the Southern California sand
I start another band
Reeling and rolling with the same hand

The gargoyle grinders making a path for
Vanilla side winders
Through the styrofoam underbelly of this dusty land

Who Dat
Touchdown
Dance

Saints Football

Raiders 14 Bowl VI?

Saints 49 Super

Badono Vojtech Luza
10-1-2021

07/20/21

STEALING THE LIGHT

They're taking my roommate Walter's call light again
Here at Grand Valley Healthcare Center in Van Nuys, CA

He may press it every five minutes
But they still cannot win it

The Polish Pegasus has a right to the call light no matter what
Even if he uses it ten times every minute

Once they burglarize it
He can sue them
Do them
Blue them
Cue them
Burn them
Or reach a compromise and
Pray for them

07/20/21
NEW YORK DREAMING

All day
Every day here at
Grand Valley Healthcare Center
In Van Nuys, CA

I dream of living in New York City
Leaving Los Angeles in the dust after 15 years

Making my way East to the teeming masses and steaming glasses
Times Square
Broadway
Macy's
Herald Square
Visitor beware on this grassy lair

First I was 23
Bipolar mental illness set me free

Then married at 35
Divorce sent me on a dive

Now engaged for ten years at 57
Or a natural air alright
This is my last chance at Manhattan heaven

Acting on the stage to Shakespeare's page
Aeschylus, Sophocles and Aristophanes too

Starting my own company at noon
Is the boon

Mime all body and soul
No hole or mole

THE LION AND THE BEAR

Here at Grand Valley Healthcare Center
In Van Nuys, CA
Two beasts make my head roam

The one with the mane
Carries a holy name

The one that sleeps has nothing to reap
But rest to keep

The former lives in the jungle
The latter in the forest

Neither like the human being for he kills
Outside of his species

Still with a will
Just to get a fill

Less and less lions
Less and less Grizzlies
More and more cryin'

I do not know if they with each other go
But have never moved slow
In finding their glow on this orb of woe

07/21/21

SITTIN' IN THE HALLWAY IN MY BLACK WHEELCHAIR

Here at Grand Valley Healthcare Center
In Van Nuys, CA

Where the air is dry
The cheerleaders don't cry
Time does not die

Dreaming has just begun
Love is on the run
Pain is no bane

Hanging out by the wall
Watching all the people fall

Listening to at least every phone call
Till at least 4

The lady from the health department
Talking to me

Crying because my 90-year-old-roommate
Recognizes me for the first time in two weeks

Being nice to the physical therapy director
Even though we do not like each other

Praying to God again that I get out of here soon
Wondering if God listens to fools like me
Who forget to drink tea

As visitors come and go
Thinking on the down low
Everybody trying but no one buying

07/22/21

UP AND DOWN ON THE NURSING HOME ROLLERCOASTER

At this old age home deciding whether to go or stay
Woe or turn gray

Place or pace
Grace or race
Ph.D or security

Flesh or mesh
Roman Catholic or Jew

Raisin or poison
End or beginning

Master or model
Leader or follower

Healthy or sick
John or Mick

Artist or teacher
Poet or writer
Wanderer or preacher

President or prophet
John or Bobby

Neon or night
Writing or reporting

Sun or moon
Gun or gloom

Knowing or going
Sewing or blowing

Patience or rain
Funeral or faith

Parents or pain
Sanity or bane

Perry Mason or Ironside
Rocky or Rambo

Broad or boney
Adult or infant

Face or trace
Lace or mace

07/23/21

BEELZEBUB'S BANK

Satan's office
Is where I work till dusk

Nothing is good enough anymore
Life is a slumbering bore

I have the self-esteem of a whore
Losing it like Al Gore

Confidence steamrolled
Vision dark as 3AM

Poison in my thoughts
Dread my lot
Cuffs already bought

Why always me?
Wanting to be free

Stuck in this insane shoe box
In December
And I am barely hanging on

I can no longer save myself
I require a magical elf
Or a miracle from some sacred self

If not
I will rot in my cot

Lying in snot
Like the world's biggest fool
Who never learned to play it cool

IN THIS POET'S NIGHTMARE

Where gargoyles come to stare
At the nearest snare

Where holding on to the past is
A scribe's blessed path

The boulevard of shattered dreams
Is paved in blood and inseams

This wordsmith's kennel boasts a most
Wretched sentinel dining on
Rat claws and eel eyes
Bat's heads and bee rinds

This versaholic's bad dream is brought to you by
Iron cages and furious rages
Torn pages and plastic stages

In this writer's tunnel
Light is coal black

Artists die of a heart attack
Arthritis stalls the young
While cancer murders the unsung

Here ideas move like turtles and
Sins like hares

After midnight time stands
As thick as a Grizzly Bear

07/23/21
ON THE LEFT

Is not the right the conservative sight?
The absurd fight?

Are the liberal knights making hay
Of an insane light?

Careening, oh, turning
Into that sad bite

Twisting and moving
Like the teenage night

Until momma and poppa
Are no longer in sight

And the non-right resurfacing like
A candle in the atmosphere ever so bright

A rebellious artist flexing his or her might
A dead movement never in flight
A narrow coat, oh, so tight

A two-party system
Now a thunderous blight

THE WAY YOU MOVE

(Dedicated to Patricia)

Like a prophet leading a flock
A docket smelling its stock
A pocket holding a rock

You sway and sashay like Elvis Presley
Move and groove like Tom Jones

Ram and jam like Prince
Kick and stick like Michael Jackson

Your lithe frame a new game
But never tame

Like your dancing feet
Hitting the asphalt street
To make life complete

07/24/21

MY FRIEND THE PHONE

Bends like a bone
Here at Grand Valley Healthcare Center
In Van Nuys, CA

This tool is white and plastic
It takes a beating and keeps on bleeding

Without it I could not keep track of the outside world
Or my beauty queen Patricia

It must have been knocked on the floor
A hundred times

But a hundred and one times
It gets back up

It turns green when it rings
And red when it sings

I believe in it and need it like air
My friend the phone is fair
It grows no hair

07/24/21
TWILIGHT

Night meeting day
Light versus gray
Here at the nursing home
Time laying still
On some barbecue grill

The Summer dancing
Above a mountain range

How strange

Lakes shimmering
In gold and bronze

Like boulevards made of bonds
Autumn knocking on the door

Sun ripping the floor
Moon gathering more
Freeway a cement whore

This balance anything
But a neon bore

SKIN VERSUS TIN

This poetry
Spilling seed onto need

Not robot or computer
Car or train
Bicycle or plane

Brain mine
Heart not on line
Soul like vine

Being is God
Words like toes
Too many to count

All sacred
A literary bridge to the maker

No faker
Or hacker

Merely the sky and clouds
Sun and earth

Poetry that gives birth
Voice without mirth

This archipelago of poverty and pain
Rescued by metaphors and similes

Of another bane
That do not harmony strain
Karma drain

07/24/21

MAKING THE BEST OF IT

I never did
For I never could

But now I can
Like a book that has been banned

Baskin Robbins' peppermint
Out of service for four years

All of this talent
Polished and infused

Motivation fueled
By confidence and faith

Networking fed by love
Which is God

Fashion led by mod
Had by nod
Grown in Cape Cod

I am flying
Will not be dying

Not to be grounded
By any sound

I make it better
By owning the sweater

Purifying the dark
By climbing bark

Answering the critics by going to bat
Life is one dead rat

07/25/21

DADDY, OH, DADDY

In my 46 years on the planet with you
We never huddled or scheduled a chat
Tit for tat

Now I realize in this old age home

How I needed a heart to heart
How I yearned for your love

I needed it like a glove
Your support and faith from above

Your two thin arms embracing mine
Squeezing me tight so I can see

Holding my hand into tomorrow
To rid me of the well-hidden
Guilt, pity and sorrow

Instead you made the pain worse
The suffering a curse

Calling me an idiot, dummy and fool
You loosened my stool
I always wondered why you needed your books
More than me

Your brain anything but free
When you died I was in Galilee

07/27/21

GURNEY GRAB

Two young men grab the sheet under me
Here at Grand Valley Healthcare Center
In Van Nuys, CA

And throw me from my bed to the gurney
Into the ambulance I go nice and slow

Like a beached whale
The aquarium in its ill-advised blow

Bumps and freeway bruises
My body loses

Maneuvering me into the dentist's chair
Like a long-lost Grizzly Bear

X-rays and chair stays until we leave the office
A cool dentist

One more ride to the nursing home
Where I am on loan until these gams feel at home

Tribute to 9/11

Cross

Catholic
Cross

CBS

NBC

ABC

FOX

NYPD

Radomir Vojtech Luza
10-1-2021

07/27/21
FIVE TIMES A WEEK

Building muscles
Like beautiful Brussels
Here at Grand Valley Healthcare Center
In Van Nuys, CA

Monday through Friday
Like the sky in May

I will find my way
And pray to the next day

Picture the finish line
Like a boulevard of Pine

Trust myself
Love what is mine

God wants me here
To believe in fine

Walker then cane
Finish the lane

Last step walking alone
Like a long trip home

To Nome
Signaling Rome

07/27/21

WHY FIGHT IT?

It is now that the Pine becomes the Maple
The line is the staple
The grind is papal

The present is
The past
The future

Don't tell me about not being nurtured
I am this country's creature
Always performing a feature

Forever in the moment
Time is the foment

Trusting the tide
Leaving my instinct at the slide

Learning not to hide
My spirit will abide
All I have is my pride

07/28/21
5:55 AM

Light through the blinds
Like water through the mines

A desperate plea to find slavery
A dogmatic pledge to begin diplomacy

Pink clouds like peppermint pounds
Blue sky like Cadillac high

Trees still as the Queen's sentries
Electric wires silent as a millionaire's Bentleys

Tenderly and calmly
The day begins gently

07/29/21

A THOUSAND WINDING BOULEVARDS LEADING TO THE DEATH OF YOUR PAIN

(For Patricia)

When I became a thousand lights
You turned green
While I was yellow

A thousand crows flew over a thousand meadows
While I only walked on one

When I became red again I merged with your blue
For when a thousand lights confuse a thousand days
Infuse a million dawns

Who am I to turn to you
And say I love you
And who are you to say it is me and you against the world

When I became orange
Autumn came and died a sudden bronze

But I cared not because I had turned pink
Next to your jackhammering spirit and rural hands
That blister dormant volcanoes

07/29/21

FRENZIED FRIDAY

The ugliness of the sky
Colored black and gray
Bleached white like May

Sand brown
Waves down

Shore donning gown
This weekday of renown
Wearing a frown

Plazas crowded
Parks re-routed

Boulevards molested
Avenues raped
Atmosphere vaped

Singing like Sinatra
Pivoting like Presley

Fifth day
Pushing my bay

The way to my pay
In this malevolent fray

07/30/21
ANOTHER 40 FEET

Here at Grand Valley Healthcare Center
In Van Nuys, CA

I walk with therapy socks and boot on right foot
Again for over 40 feet

And no one is in my shoes
And no one understands
My painful right leg and severe
Arthritis in both shoulders

The will it requires to prepare
Patience to crawl 4x10
On both meanderers

When I turn into an animal
My eyes are ketchup red
My hands solar bronze

These ten fingers grasping hold of victory over myself
Of the doubt that perishes when God gets between you and fear

Of the careening car once crashed and smashed
Now perfect and bound
Confident in sight and sound
Color and ground on top of the pitcher's mound

BOOK SUMMARY

This light, this sword, this sabre, this Great White Shark, this grand collection of poetry, then, eats its way through any hole or depression.

It is the sun to the disappearing moon, Jupiter to Mars, living in paradise not behind bars.

Written in and around Grand Valley Healthcare Center, the nursing home in Van Nuys, CA where Luza has spent the last ten or so months, this landmark autobiographical poetry collection embraces the pain, suffering, frustration, longing and suicidal tendencies that come with a true artist's imprisonment in one of these facilities.

So, freedom chained, love aborted and harmony molested, here he is swinging for any fence he can find.

If the questions are:
Why is human kind on earth?
Where did we come from?
What does it mean to be human?

Then, NURSING HOME BLUES has the answers spiritually, philosophically, metaphysically, emotionally, intellectually and psychologically.

Tomorrow is a blue dawn, yesterday a red maple and today a green meadow.

This tome is a buffet for poets and a cornucopia for writers and thinkers alike.

Do not put it down!!

Printed in the United States
by Baker & Taylor Publisher Services